STRATEGIC SOCIAL MEDIA MARKETING:

Unlocking the Secrets to Viral Success

Copyright Notice

© 2024 Augustine Paul. All rights reserved.

This material may not be reproduced, displayed, modified or distributed without the written permission of the copyright owner. Request permission by contacting the Author.

Table of Contents

- Title …………………..…….…1
- Copyright Notice………...……..2
- Table of content……..….……....3
- Chapter 1…....…. ………...4 - 18
- Chapter 2……..….…………19 - 24
- Chapter 3……..….…………25 - 33
- Chapter 4……..….…………34 - 38
- Chapter 5……..….…………39 - 50
- Chapter 6……..….…………51 - 54
- Chapter 7…....…………….55 - 57
- Chapter 8……………...………58 - 61
- Chapter 9……………...……62 - 67
- Chapter 10…………………68 - 69

Chapter 1:

Introduction to Social Media Marketing

Social networks are an interactive technology that facilitates the creation, exchange and integration of content, ideas, interests and other expressions through virtual communities and networks.

In the context of media, the word "social" suggests that platforms enable social activity. Social media can enhance and expand your network. Users access social networks through web-based applications or customized applications on mobile devices. These interactive platforms allow individuals, communities and organizations to share, co-author, discuss, interact and curate personalized or user-generated content. Social media is used to record memories, learn, and make friends. They can be used to promote people, companies, products, and ideas. Social media can be used to feed, publish, or share news. Popular social media platforms with over 100 million registered users include Twitter, Facebook, WeChat, ShareChat, Instagram, Pinterest, QZone, Weibo, VK, Tumblr, Baidu Tieba, and LinkedIn. Some popular platforms that are often referred to as social media services, depending on the interpretation, include YouTube, Letterboxd, QQ, Quora, Telegraph, WhatsApp, Signal, LINE, Snapchat, Pinterest, Viber, Reddit, Discord, TikTok, and Microsoft Teams. . Wikis are an example of collaborative content creation. Social media differ from traditional media (such as newspapers, television, and radio) in many ways, including quality, reach, frequency, availability, relevance, and persistence. Social media use a dialogue distribution system (multiple sources to many receivers), while traditional media use a mono distribution model (one source to many receivers). For example, a newspaper would be distributed to a large number of subscribers, while a radio station would broadcast the same program in a city. Observers point out that social media has a variety of positive and negative effects. Social media helps increase a person's sense of connection with others and serves as an effective communication (or marketing) tool for businesses, entrepreneurs, nonprofit organizations, advocacy groups, political parties, and governments. Social movements use social networks to communicate and organize. Social media has been criticized for a variety of negative effects on children and young people, including exposure to inappropriate content, abuse from adults, sleep problems, attention problems, feelings of exclusion and various mental health disorders.

The PLATO system was introduced at the University of Illinois in the 1960s and was later sold commercially by Control Data Corporation. It provided the first forms of social networking functionality, including

Articles (a PLATO messaging forum application), TERM talk (an instant messaging article), Talkomatic (perhaps the first online chat room), News Report (a newspaper in crowdsourcing line) and Blogs and Access. A list that allows the owner of an article file or other application to restrict access to a specific group of users, such as friends, classmates, or colleagues only.

ARPANET came to the Internet in 1967, and in the late 1970s enabled the exchange and communication of non-governmental/commercial ideas, as shown in the MIT Artificial Intelligence Laboratory's 1982 Computing Handbook illustrated by netiquette (or "netiquette"). . described in . ARPANET was developed for the Internet in the 1990s. Conceived in 1979 by Tom Truscott and Jim Ellis at the University of North Carolina at Chapel Hill and Duke University, Usenet was the first social networking application. and was launched in 1980.

In 1973, Public Memory, the precursor to the electronic bulletin board system (BBS), was launched. On February 16, 1978, the Chicago Computer Bulletin Board System was launched, marking the beginning of the emergence of traditional BBSs. Before long, most major cities in the United States had more than one BBS, running on TRS-80, Apple II, Atari, IBM PC, Commodore 64, Sinclair, and similar computers. CompuServe, Prodigy, and AOL were the three largest BBS companies and were among the first to migrate to the Internet in the 1990s. From the mid-1980s to the mid-1990s, there were tens of thousands of BBSs in North America alone. Message boards were an iconic BBS in the 1980s and early 1990s. In 1991, Tim Berners-Lee combined HTML hypertext software with the Internet to create the World Wide Web. This success led to the proliferation of blogs, listservs, and email services.

Message boards have migrated to the web and evolved into Internet forums, supported by factors including economic access and the ability to serve large numbers of people at once. In the 21st century, these early text-based programs have expanded to include images and videos with the help of digital cameras and camera phones.

With the advent of Web 2.0, online services have evolved from a networked communication channel to an interactive social media platform. Social media began in the mid-1990s with platforms such as GeoCities, Classmates.com, and SixDegrees.com. While instant messaging and chat clients already existed at the time, SixDegrees was unique because it was the first online service designed to allow people to connect using their real names rather than anonymity. It has features like personal profiles, friend lists, and school relationships, and is "the first place to connect with people." The platform's name was inspired by the idea of "six levels of separation," suggesting that each person on earth has only six connections to one other person. A 2015 study reported that global users spend 22% of their online time on social networks, likely due to the proliferation of smartphones. By 2023, the number of people using social media will reach 4.76 billion, representing 59% of the world's population.

Social media marketing is the use of social media platforms and websites to promote products or services. Although terms like e-marketing and digital marketing still dominate academia, social media marketing is gaining popularity among practitioners and researchers.

Most social media platforms (think: Facebook, LinkedIn, Instagram, social media marketing. Businesses use social media marketing to address issues with a variety of stakeholders, including current and potential customers, current and potential employees, journalists, bloggers, and the general public. On a technical level, social media marketing includes managing marketing campaigns, governance, setting boundaries (such as continued or continued use), and establishing "culture" and "tone." " of social networks. the needs of the company. Using social media marketing, businesses can allow consumers and Internet users to post user-generated content (e.g., online reviews, product reviews, etc.), known as " earned media" instead of using suppliers. . Preparation of advertising texts.

Social media can be a useful source of market information and a way to hear your customers' opinions. Blogs, content communities, and forums are platforms where people share reviews and recommendations about brands, products, and services. Businesses can leverage and analyze customer voice and feedback generated on social media for marketing purposes. In this way, social media is an inexpensive source of marketing intelligence that marketers and managers can use to track and respond to identified customer problems and uncover marketing opportunities. For example, the Internet is full of videos and images of "bending tests" of the iPhone 6 showing that the coveted phone can be bent with manual pressure. The so-called "Bendgate" controversy has left consumers waiting months for the latest iPhones to be tampered with. However, Apple issued a statement from the start saying that this problem is very rare and that the company has taken several steps to make the casing of mobile devices more durable. Unlike traditional market research methods such as surveys, focus groups, and data mining, which are time-consuming and labor-intensive and can take weeks or months to analyze, marketers can use social media to capture "real-time" information about consumer behavior and perceptions of the company's brand or products. This is very useful in today's highly dynamic, competitive, and fast-paced global commerce.

  Social media can be used not only as a public relations and direct marketing tool, but also as a communication channel, targeting specific audiences using influencers and social media personalities as effective tools to engage customers. This strategy is widely known as influencer marketing. Influencer marketing gives brands the opportunity to reach their target audience in an honest and authentic way by advertising their products or services through a special group of selected influencers. In fact, brands will spend up to $15 billion on influencer marketing by 2022, according to Business Insider Intelligence estimates based on data from Mediakix. Technologies that previously existed in public media, such as television broadcasts and newspapers, can also provide advertisers with a suitable target audience, since advertisements placed during sports broadcasts or in the sports sections of newspapers are more likely to be read by sports fans.

However, social networking sites can target precisely niche markets. Using digital tools like Google AdSense, advertisers can target ads to specific groups of people, such as people interested in social media, political campaigns related to certain groups, or video games. Google AdSense does this by searching for keywords in social media users' Internet posts and comments. It would be difficult for a television station or print newspaper to offer targeted advertising (but not impossible, as demonstrated by the specific topic of the "Special Issues" section, which newspapers can use to sell targeted advertising). In many cases, social networks are considered an excellent tool to avoid expensive market research. They are characterized by providing a brief, quick and direct way to reach the audience through the use of well-known characters. For example, an athlete endorsed by a sportswear company also attracts millions of people who are interested in what they do or how they compete and now want to be a part of that athlete endorsing that company. Customers used to go to stores to see their products in collaboration with famous athletes, but now you can see the latest clothes from famous athletes like Cristiano Ronaldo online with the click of a button.

She promotes clothing directly through her Twitter, Instagram and Facebook accounts. Facebook and LinkedIn are leading social media platforms where users can target their ads to a large extent. Hypertargeting uses not only public profile information, but also information entered by the user but hidden from others. There are many examples of companies starting some type of online conversation with the community to build relationships with customers.

According to Constantinides, Lorenzo, and Gómez Borja (2008), "Companies such as Sun Microsystems Chairman and CEO Jonathan Swartz, Apple Computer CEO Steve Jobs, and McDonald's Vice Chairman Bob Langat regularly blog of the CEO to encourage customers to interact and freely express their feelings, thoughts, suggestions or ideas about the publication, the company or its products.In recent years, algorithm-based social networks have become popular.

.One of the social media platforms that uses this. It's strategy is TikTok and it now has around 1.5 billion users, most of whom are children and teenagers. The algorithms used on the platform encourage. creativity among TikTok users, as the platform's overall reach and challenges change every day. Thanks to this feature, content creators, regardless of their size, can go viral by appearing on the "For You" page. " from TikTok. The page's "Recommended for You" algorithm allows users to recommend videos to you based on your previous views, likes, and shares. This is very beneficial for small businesses that use the platform as a means of social media marketing. While they may be starting small, following trends, using hashtags, and more, anyone can promote themselves on this emerging app to reach new audiences around the world. Additionally, the use of algorithm-driven content on TikTok can generate positive user response rates, as the target audience tends to be younger users who are more susceptible to these increasingly complex marketing communications. With this in mind, TikTok is full of rich content, including images and videos, which can benefit influencer marketing compared to text-based platforms, which are less engaging for audiences.

Potential benefits of social media marketing include;

It allows businesses to market to large, diverse audiences that cannot be reached through traditional marketing methods, such as telephone and email marketing. .

Marketing on most social media platforms costs next to nothing, making them accessible to almost any business.

It is suitable for single and direct marketing to target groups and markets.

Businesses can interact directly with customers, allowing them to get feedback and resolve issues quickly.

The perfect place for companies to carry out market research.

It can be used as a way to obtain information about the competition and improve competitive advantage.

Social platforms can be used to promote events, prices and brand news.

Social platforms can be used to offer rewards in the form of points and discounts.

Allows companies to create online platforms to promote and sell their products.

It can be used to find potential customers and give them the opportunity to do business.

Build a community to improve your business' presence in your target market.

Chapter 2:
Setting Clear Goals and Objectives

SMART The framework is commonly used in a variety of fields, including project management, employee performance management, and personal development. This term was coined by George T. Doran argued in the November 1981 issue of Management Review that he advocated setting Specific, Measurable, Assignable, Realistic, Time-bound objectives, hence the acronym S.M.A.R.T.

Since its inception, the SMART framework has continued to evolve, leading to the emergence of several variations of the acronym. Commonly used translations include "achievable," "appropriate," and "timely." In addition, some authors introduce additional letters in the acronyms. For example, some refer to SMART goals, which include

19

"self-definition," while others use SMARTER goals. and several other places. This framework allows the goal setter to know exactly what to expect and the evaluator to have specific criteria for evaluation. The acronym SMART is related to Peter Drucker's concept of management by objectives (MBO), indicating its central role in strategic planning and operational management.

In this digital age, social media has become an important tool for businesses of all sizes. Whether you're a small startup or a large enterprise, having a strong social media presence can help you reach a broader audience, build customer relationships, and drive sales. However, while social media can be a powerful tool, it's important to ensure your efforts align with business goals and objectives. One of the key ways to align your social media efforts with your business goals is to clearly define those goals. For example, if your goal is to increase brand awareness, you should focus on building followers and creating content that reflects your brand and its values. If your goal is to drive sales, you need to create content that encourages people to buy. By clearly defining your goals and objectives, you can ensure that your social media efforts are effective in achieving those objectives. Another key factor to consider when aligning your social media efforts with your business goals is understanding your target audience. This includes understanding demographics, interests, behaviors, and where they spend their time online. By understanding your target audience, you can create content that resonates with them and is more likely to generate engagement. Another effective way to combine social media with overall business goals is through a social media marketing campaign. Well-planned and executed campaigns can help you achieve certain goals, such as increasing website traffic, increasing engagement, and driving sales. For example, a new product launch event could include pre-launch teas on social media, live product demonstrations on Instagram or Facebook Live, and post-launch promotions with special offers for event shoppers. Additionally, social media analytics can help you track the performance of your campaigns and make adjustments as needed. By analyzing engagement, click, and conversion rates, you can learn which strategies work and which don't. This can help you make data-driven decisions about your social media strategy and ultimately help you achieve your business goals. Another strategy for connecting social media efforts to overall business goals is to use influencer marketing. Partnering with influencers in your industry can help you reach a broader audience and build your brand's credibility. For example, if you are a clothing brand and you collaborate with a popular fashion blog, their followers will see your brand with their own eyes and may purchase. In short, aligning your social media efforts with your overall business goals and objectives is critical to success. By clearly defining your goals, understanding your target audience, developing social media marketing campaigns, leveraging analytics, and working with influencers, you can ensure your social media efforts are achieving your business goals. By following these strategies, companies can see a significant improvement in their social ROI and ultimately grow their business.

Make Goal setting a case study. Goal setting involves developing a plan of action designed to motivate and guide an individual or group toward achieving a goal. Goals are more reflective than fleeting desires and goals. Therefore, setting a goal means that one invests thoughts, feelings, and behavior in achieving the goal. In doing so, the goal setter establishes a desired future state that is different from the current state, thus creating a contrast that will then motivate future actions. Goal setting can be guided by goal setting standards (or principles), such as the SMART standards. Goal setting is an important part of the management and personal development literature. Research by Edwin A. Locke and his colleagues (especially Gary Latham) shows that specific, ambitious goals improve performance more than simple or general goals. Ideally, weight goals should be set at the 90th percentile of performance, assuming that it is motivation rather than ability that makes it difficult to achieve this level of performance.

As long as a person accepts the goal, has the ability to achieve it, and there are no conflicting goals, there is a positive linear relationship between goal difficulty and job performance.

Chapter 3:
Understanding Your Target Audience

In order to understand the audience that are going to patronize your business, you need to carry out market research. Market research is a systematic effort to gather information about target markets and customers – understanding them, starting with who they are. It is an important part of business strategy and the most important factor in maintaining competitiveness. Market research helps identify and analyze market needs, market size and competition.

The technique includes both technical methods such as focus groups, in-depth interviews and ethnography, as well as quantitative techniques such as consumer research and secondary data analysis. Includes social and opinion research, which is the systematic collection and interpretation of information about people or organizations using statistical and analytical methods of applied social sciences to obtain knowledge or support decision making. Market research, marketing research and advertising are all business activities. These activities are sometimes treated unfairly. Although both involve consumers, marketing research focuses primarily on marketing processes such as sales performance and sales force performance, while marketing research focuses mainly on sales and distribution. Two explanations for the confusion between marketing research and marketing research are that the terminology is similar and marketing research is a subset of marketing research. This creates more confusion as large companies have experience and practice in both areas.

Another way to understand your audience is by creating a buyer persona. A persona in user-centered design and marketing (also known as a user, user persona, customer persona, client persona) is a fictional character designed to represent people who might use a website, brand, or product in a similar way to a user type. Personas represent similarities across consumer groups or sectors. They are based on demographic and behavioral information collected from users, qualitative interviews and participant observation. Personas are one of the outcomes of market segmentation, where marketers use the results of statistical analysis and qualitative observations to draw profiles of people, giving them names and personalities to paint a picture of who they might be in real life. The term persona is used widely in technology and Internet applications, as well as in advertising, where other terms such as pencil portraits may be used.

Personas are useful in considering the goals, wants, and limitations of a brand's customers and users to help guide decisions about a service, product, or interface (such as the functionality, communication, and visual design of a website). Personas can be used as a tool in the user-centered software design process. They can introduce the principles of collaborative design to areas such as business design and Internet marketing. A user persona is a representation of the goals and behaviors of an imagined set of users. In most cases, personas are compiled from data collected through user interviews or surveys. They are included in brief descriptions of the article that include behavioral patterns, goals, skills, attitudes and fictional details of the person to make them a real person. In addition to human-computer interaction (HCI), personas are widely used in marketing, sales, and process design. Personas provide common behaviors, opinions, and possible objections of people associated with a particular person.

According to Pruitt and Adlin, using people in product development has many benefits. Humans are psychologically interesting because they put a human face on consumer data. By thinking about the needs of fictional people, designers can better understand what real people might want. This concept can help in brainstorming, using case description and point description. Pruitt and Adlin argue that it is easier for people to communicate with engineering teams, allowing engineers, developers and others to integrate customer data in an acceptable way. They cited many examples of personas used for communication in various development projects. People also help avoid common design mistakes. The first is to create what Cooper calls "elastic users," meaning that different stakeholders can define "users" based on their convenience when making product decisions. Defining personas helps the team have a shared understanding of the goals, strengths, and backgrounds of real users. Personas help prevent "self-inflicted design," where a designer or developer may unwittingly produce his or her own mental model of a product's design, which may differ greatly from the mental model of the target group. Personas can provide a reality check by helping designers focus their designs on the target situations that users are likely to encounter, rather than the rare events that target personas rarely encounter.

According to Cooper, edge cases that need to be handled naturally and efficiently should not be a design consideration. Data about groups can be contextualized, understood, and remembered in a coherent narrative. Recommended solutions can be tailored to meet individual user needs. Prioritization can be based on how well the attributes meet the requirements of one or more roles. Give a human "face" to create empathy for human beings. Help support better design choices by narrowing the designer's focus. Helps understand what drives the audience to learn more about the product/service. At this time performance will vary depending on the needs of the project, all people put the main focus on potential users.

Audience segmentation is the process of dividing people into equal subgroups based on established criteria such as product usage, demographics, psychographics, communication behavior, and media usage. Audience segmentation is used in commercial marketing so that advertisers can design and create products and services that meet the needs of target groups. In social marketing, the audience is divided into small groups and assumed to have similar interests, needs, and behaviors. This concept allows social marketers to design appropriate social or health messages that influence people to take recommended actions. Audience segmentation is widely recognized as an important strategy for communication campaigns affecting health and social change. Audience segmentation can make campaigns more effective when the message is tailored to different sub-segments, and campaigns are more effective when target audiences are selected based on sentiment and receptivity.

    The driver of an audience segmentation strategy is the development of criteria that can be used to create similar groups. Commonly used criteria are demographics (age, educational level, income, race, and gender) and geography (region, county, census tract). Because the audience is made up solely of demographic characteristics (such as young Asian Americans), they form a large group with diverse beliefs, values, and behaviors, demographic characteristics may not be sufficient as a distinguishing criterion. Sophisticated segmentation strategies use psychosocial, behavioral and psychographic aspects (personality, values, attitudes, interests, willingness to change and lifestyle) as variables to segment audience groups. Once the audience has been segmented based on selected criteria, campaigns are designed and communication channels are selected to effectively reach the target audience. Grunig's segmentation model Grunig proposed a theoretical segmentation model consisting of a series of internal and external nests. The inner nest contains ;individuals (individual communication behavior and consequences) and communities (groups of people with similar interests and problems). The outer nest consists of community, psychological, lifestyle, subcultural and social relationships, geodemographics, demographic categories, and demography. As nesting moves toward the inner center, nesting shows increasing precision rather than universality, providing the audience with more details and insights, allowing the communication campaign to create more accurate content for the target audience.

Take for example the trendsetting brands, Their campaign features Colin Kaepernick, who has gone viral for his bravery on social issues. In keeping with trending topics, Nike appeals not only to the existing audience but to a broader audience as well.

Wendy's Their witty and often direct tweets have made them a standout on the platform. Wendy's Burgers promotes trending topics to engage with fans in an authentic and fun way, keeping the brand at the forefront.

Glossier's success is largely due to its ability to leverage popular content and connect with its community. By using user-generated content and interacting directly with audiences on platforms like

Instagram, Glossier has built a loyal customer base that actively engages in communication.

Chapter 4:
Selecting the Right Social Media Platforms

Social media has become a part of modern communication, with many platforms available to suit all needs and preferences. Below is an overview of the most popular social media platforms;

Facebook – With over 2 billion active users, Facebook is the largest social media platform. It's popular with all ages and offers a wide range of business features, including Facebook Pages, Groups, and Ads. It's important to remember how people use Facebook: to build relationships and keep in touch with old friends. This makes Facebook a great platform for building loyalty among your existing customer base. One downside to Facebook is that it can be difficult to reach a new audience; When evaluating Facebook as a potential platform, carefully consider your business objectives. If you're trying to grow a new business, Facebook may not be the best option, but if you're building a loyal following and need a way to stay in touch with them, this could be a great option for your business. .

Instagram is a photo and video sharing platform with more than one billion active users. Instagram is one of the fastest growing platforms, especially among young people. Like Pinterest, Instagram relies on photos or videos to create conversations. Therefore, the platform is ideal for image-based businesses such as art, food, retail and beauty. Being a growing platform, there is less noise than Facebook. This means that the platform is useful for generating leads because it has a broader reach.

Twitter is a microblogging platform that allows users to send short messages or "tweets" of up to 280 characters. It's popular with journalists, politicians and public figures, and is perfect for businesses looking to have real-time conversations. Twitter is a great platform to increase brand awareness. Twitter uses hashtags to organize conversations around words or phrases. By searching for hashtags, you can find out what people are talking about so you can tweet and participate in popular conversations. The main reason is because Twitter can provide information about trending topics, media outlets often use Twitter to search for news. Since Twitter is often used to provide real-time updates to audiences, many brands combine Twitter and offline interactions such as events.

LinkedIn is a social media platform with more than 700 million users. LinkedIn is the most used site among adults. A large number of its users are in the age group of 30 to 49 years. LinkedIn is also unique because it has a narrow focus. People use LinkedIn to find jobs and make professional connections. Therefore, the platform can be used for B2B lead generation, general networking, and recruiting.

YouTube is a video sharing platform with more than 2 billion active users. Although YouTube has 2.3 billion users, its reach goes much further. It is not necessary to register as a user to view content on YouTube. As a result, YouTube has become one of the largest search engine platforms. Most searches are related to "how-to" videos. Service companies that can provide this type of content, as well as educational and lifestyle videos, do well on this platform. It's ideal for businesses that want to share video content and is popular with younger audiences.

TikTok is a video sharing platform with more than one billion active users. TikTok is famous for its short videos. Like Pinterest and Instagram, TikTok is best suited for visually-based industries such as art, food, retail, beauty, and other service industries. TikTok's user base is very small. The platform helps target the 18-24 age group and build brand awareness. It's great for businesses looking to create short video content and is popular with younger audiences.

Pinterest is a visual discovery platform with more than 400 million active users. Pinterest is used for "scrapbooking" or, in other words, for saving content by "pinning" photos or videos to a bulletin board. Pinterest's user base is dominated by women. Some of the most popular pins include recipes, styling ideas, eye-catching photos, and DIY techniques. Since Pinterest is a visual platform, it needs powerful graphics to attract users. Successful adoption of Pinterest advertising is associated with strong sales. It is suitable for companies that want to showcase their products and services and is popular with women.

Each social media platform offers unique features and demographics, and businesses should choose the platform that best suits their needs and goals.

Chapter 5:

Crafting a Winning Content Strategy

As marketers, we understand that social media is essential to an effective marketing strategy. With so many social networks available to us, it is important to stay organized and plan when and what to share; This is where a social media calendar comes into play. Before we get into our list of the best tools to stay organized, here's what you need to know about social media calendars and why they're important.

A social media content calendar is a summary of your upcoming posts organized by date and time. A social media calendar can be a spreadsheets, a digital calendar, or an interactive dashboard. You can also use the content calendar to schedule your social media posts, schedule content or posts in advance, write blog posts, emails, and more. A popular piece of advice given to new bloggers is to "just get started"! This tip is great for blogging for fun or as a hobby. However, if your blog is for commercial purposes or you want to use it for income, give the blog some thought. This article states that up to 63% of companies do not have a written strategy, so they resort to improving headlines and adopting an automated approach. Another article states that according to the Content Marketing Institute, 60% of marketers with social media and a written public strategy are considered more effective, compared to 32% of marketers with only a verbal strategy. Content calendar is a common tool for all experienced bloggers and content creators. Since social media accounts are important to social media presence, some businesses hire a social media manager to help them determine the type of visual content they need for a social media calendar template.

Here are some benefits of having a Content Calendar;

Keep It Organized and Tracked – A detailed schedule is essential to keeping your blog organized and organized (and maintaining your sanity). A good marketing plan includes strategy and a good marketing plan includes content. It keeps you focused and your content is consistent with your overall plan.

Good brainstorming – A common objection when encouraging clients to blog is what topic will meet the needs of their target audience. This is another area where a content calendar is essential. It's a great tool for generating ideas to create blog posts or other content that will resonate with your target audience.

Helps maintain consistency – After a few months of creating content, they stop because they run out of ideas or lose their original focus. An editorial calendar helps you maintain consistency in creating and publishing content. It helps keep the audience interested. For example, subscribers to my blog know that until last year I published a weekly sales summary every Friday. It helps keep your attention on my content.

keys to staying informed – As an entrepreneur or business owner, it is important to stay informed about what is happening in your business and your business. Using a calendar can help you stay up to date with the latest news from the web and social media.

Helps Reduce Daily Stress However, using a content calendar for social media activities can help you or your marketing/social media team create some order in a chaotic day and reduce your daily stress.

Therefore, your fans and followers on each social network can have a balanced mix of informative and entertaining content to keep them interested. A social media calendar tool also ensures that you don't fall into the trap of posting the same type of content on all social media channels. If you publish the same content, using the content calendar template created in Google Sheets will help you change each piece of content to fit the right social network. This is important for your social media strategy.

Content media is a brand's fundamental asset to convey its message to its audience. Content media types include documents and articles published by providers regardless of format, angle, perspective, and purpose.

Articles – You can do this like a traditional newspaper or magazine article. As content marketing god Joe Pulizzi says, companies are now publishers. Therefore, marketers can borrow ideas from the traditional world of advertising to better engage with their audience.

Blog Posts – Blog content can come from many different angles (how to, lists, questions, why, etc.) and is often used to educate potential clients. Blog posts, usually at least 1,500 words, help your audience solve problems for themselves, allow them to do their jobs well (and then give them more reasons to use the product or service you sell). Studies have found that people who blog regularly are more likely to achieve their goals.

Websites and Landing Pages, Some call it brochure content – this content sits a little deeper in the funnel and is used to educate potential customers about how your product or service solves their challenges. This may include eCommerce product pages, etc. According to research compiled by MarketingProfs, most people are likely to research 13 pieces of content before making a purchasing decision, making this type of content extremely powerful in influencing sales. Landing pages help you share the benefits of your products, services, and content while increasing visitor conversion rates. This can include testimonials, case studies and statistics to inform your potential customers what opportunities they are missing out on if they don't use the product you sell.

Books – Joe Pulizzi famously said, "Books can be the best content marketing tool to position you or your company as a leading expert in your industry."We couldn't agree more. Publishing a book is a great way to engage with your audience and generate more business and publishing opportunities. And it doesn't take much effort: your book can be a natural extension of your content marketing strategy. Analyze your previous content (articles, whitepapers, videos, etc.) to see what topics your audience likes and wants, then go deeper and broader on those concepts in your book. The easiest way to start writing an eBook is to reuse existing content by selecting existing blog posts that perform well.

Forms – Forms are not the first thing that comes to mind when talking about types of content, but they are very useful for capturing visitor information and generating leads. Contact forms, quote request forms, inquiry forms, service selection forms etc.

Pop-ups – speaking of pop-ups, have you ever opened/scrolled a web page and seen a small window suddenly appear on your screen? That's the popup window. It can contain notifications, surveys, discount codes or, if you want something more practical, a winning wheel and countdown timer.

Well, an efficient strategy for understanding your audience is by engaging them. Before you can effectively engage your audience, you need to know who that audience is. Creating and researching your customer personas is a great way to gain insight into your target market. Buyer personas are fictional characters that represent different segments of your target audience and answer the following questions:
- What are my customers' pain points, goals, and motivations? What social platforms do they spend time on? Why do they follow our brand on social networks?
- What responses or values do you hope to get? What type of content are they associated with?
- If you've never created a customer persona for your customer base, click here for a simple guide to get started.

Once you've created your customer persona, spend time working on it until you feel like you know your customer like you know their closest family members. Remember to regularly communicate with your audience through surveys, polls and questionnaires. Your customers will change over time and this is the best way to ensure you stay relevant and attract followers and customers.

When you create content to share online, it's easy to forget that there is a real person on the other side of the screen reading what you've written. When writing a post, article, or email, always think about your customer and write your copy as if you were having a one-on-one conversation with these people. This will help ensure that you sound genuine and helpful, rather than distant or condescending. Consumers will choose an authorized and useful company, not one or the other. Your digital content marketing should show what you know, but if you use "marketing" language or confusing business jargon, customers won't find it useful.

That's why it's important to provide value while maintaining a conversational tone. When you do this, customers will see you as knowledgeable and approachable – ultimately more worthy of their trust and business.

Have you ever been interrupted at dinner by someone who talks endlessly about themselves but shows no interest in you or your ideas? If so, you probably remember how quickly you got bored, ignored them, and started looking for ways to escape. The same thing happens when brands forget to leverage digital marketing to keep a conversation going. Effective communication always starts with listening to your target market. Practice social listening, pay attention to comments and mentions on social networks. What do your customers say about you and your content? What kind of questions will your followers ask, not only about your profile, but also about your competitors and their content? When you take the time to practice careful listening and keep these questions in mind, you can learn all kinds of information about your customers. As you listen carefully and record what you read, consider how you can be creative and provide the answers your customers want. Responding to common customer requests in your digital marketing strategy will always generate greater impact and engagement.

People buy from brands they trust and trust brands that continue to evolve. One way to do this is to shape your followers' expectations about how often they receive your messages in their feed or inbox. Don't bite off more than you can chew, promise new content every day if you can't deliver. Instead, decide how often you can provide valuable content and schedule your blog posts, social media updates, video content, podcasts, or email newsletters accordingly. The cadence you choose is up to you, but the important thing is to keep your customers interested. If you only attract people when you want to increase sales, your potential customers will understand this and avoid your content, which will look like an advertisement in disguise. On the other hand, the commitment to consistency should not be an excuse to sacrifice quality for quantity. A consistent presence also means that your digital marketing content is relevant to your target audience. Instead of producing new content to meet a schedule, take the time to ensure that everything you produce has a purpose and is well executed. When you can consistently create high-quality content at a pace your customers can predict, you not only introduce your brand to your target customers, you reinforce the idea that you can continue to provide solutions. , support and services.

Chapter 6:

Analytics and Metrics

A key performance indicator (KPI) is a measure used to evaluate an organization's performance in achieving its strategic objectives. KPIs help reduce the complexity associated with performance tracking by reducing a large number of metrics to a few "important" performance indicators. KPIs are important for monitoring the performance of the individual against specific objectives. They are a reliable measurement tool that aids in decision making and provides valuable information on efficiency and productivity. Key performance indicators vary depending on the individual's operating principles, business, and objectives. They allow Content creators to accurately assess progress and make informed strategic decisions.

Tracking KPIs has four main benefits on the social media marketing :
- They provide clarity and focus in defining and communicating the vision, mission, and objectives of a Social Media Marketer.
- They also help coordinate the activities and efforts of various groups and individuals with an overall plan and direction.
- An easy way to track the performance of your content . KPIs help identify strengths, weaknesses, opportunities, threats and areas that need improvement or attention. Helps make decisions by providing information and evidence to support decisions based on real data.
- They foster a culture of responsibility that increases productivity throughout the content. This sense of responsibility and ownership by employees and managers can foster a

culture of learning and innovation where feedback and suggestions are welcomed and accepted.
There are some widely accepted Social media analysis tools. They are as follows;

1. Google Analytics
   - Features: Track traffic, user behavior, conversion rate, and social media posts.
   - Objective: Measure the impact of social work on website traffic and conversions.

2. Sprout Social
   - Features: Social listening, engagement tracking and performance reporting.
   - Usage: Manage brand mentions, analyze audience demographics, and generate reports.

3. Hootsuite
   - Features: Management, planning and analysis of social networks.
   - Usage: Schedule posts, track engagement metrics, and generate performance reports.

- Uses: schedule posts, analyze engagement, plan collaborative content.

2. Follow
   - Features: Content Calendar, Instagram Analytics, and linkedin.bio.
   - Usage: Schedule posts, track Instagram performance, and drive traffic.
3. CoSchedule -
   - Features: Marketing Calendar, Scheduling, and Analytics.
   - Usage: Plan campaigns, track performance, optimize content strategy.

Chapter 7:

Stay on Top of Trends

Identify and Align with Social Media Standards - In the ever-changing world of social media, staying on top of trends is essential for brands and influencers to remain relevant and engaged.

The first step is to identify emerging trends. This can be accomplished in a variety of ways, such as by first monitoring social media platforms. Regularly check the trending sections on platforms like Twitter, Instagram, TikTok, and LinkedIn. Tools like Google Trends and social media listening tools (e.g., Hootsuite, Sprout Social) can help determine which topics are gaining traction.

Following industry leaders and influencers is another way to adapt to social media trends. Influencers and business leaders are often trendsetters. Tracking their activities can provide insight into future trends.

Engage your audience by paying attention to what your audience is saying and how they interact with your content. Polls, surveys, and direct feedback can provide valuable insights into what they like and dislike. Once you've identified a favorite, the next step is to edit it. This includes integrating these trends into your content strategy in a way that aligns with your brand's voice and goals. Adaptation requires creativity and flexibility, allowing you to test new ideas while maintaining brand consistency.

A Content creator can test new features and formats to stay ahead of trends. Social media platforms are constantly innovating with new features and formats to keep users engaged. For brands, using these new tools can be a game-changer. Here are some ways to successfully test it out;

Being the first to use something new can give you a competitive advantage. Whether it's Instagram Reels, TikTok's interactive features, or LinkedIn Stories, early adoption can position your brand as a pioneer.

Differentiate Your Content from other people's content. Don't be afraid to differentiate your content. Experiment with videos, live streams, polls, quizzes, and interactive posts to see what resonates best with your audience.

Run A/B tests using different formats and features to find out what content works best. Analyzing these results can help refine your strategy and optimize future content.

Partnerships and Collaborations can help your content. Partnering with influencers or other brands can increase your reach and introduce your content to new audiences. Collaborative efforts can also provide new insights and new content ideas.

Chapter 8:

Competitive Analysis

In the digital age, social media has become an important platform for businesses to engage with their audience, build brand awareness, and drive sales. Monitoring your competitors' social media practices can provide valuable insights that can inform your marketing efforts.

This chapter discusses how to effectively monitor your competitors, identify opportunities and threats, and use this information to measure and differentiate yourself.

Identifying Opportunities and Threats Understanding Competitor Activities To identify opportunities and threats, it's important to understand your competitors' behavior on social media. This includes tracking their posts, engagement metrics, content strategy, and overall performance. Tools like Hootsuite, Sprout Social, and Brandwatch can make this process easier by providing detailed analysis and competitor comparisons.

Content analysis is very important. Analyze the type of content your competitors are publishing. Are they looking for video content, blogs, infographics, or user-generated content? Identifying gaps in their content strategy can highlight the chances for your brand to stand out.

Negotiate by visiting contest posts. High engagement can indicate a successful content strategy, while low engagement can indicate an area where they are struggling. This information can inform your content planning to exploit their weaknesses.

Test the sentiment of comments and engagement on your competitors' posts. Positive emotions can reveal what affects your audience, while negative emotions can reveal potential pitfalls and areas to avoid.

Identifying opportunities involves identifying gaps in the market that are not being exploited by competitors. This may include type of content, topics, engagement tactics, or platform usage. SUMMARY Tools like Google Trends and social media platforms can help keep track of trending topics and hashtags.

Unresolved Lawsuits - Pay attention to customer comments and questions about your competitors' posts. Unanswered questions or ongoing problems may be a sign that your brand can solve a need.

Influencer Collaboration - Monitor your competitors' influencers and identify untapped influencers aligned with your brand. Building relationships with these influencers can provide a competitive advantage.

Identifying threats involves identifying aspects of your competitor's strategy that could harm your efforts or your position in the market.

Keep an eye out for any aggressive marketing campaigns launched by your competitors. These activities can temporarily divert audience attention and market share. Develop prevention strategies to mitigate their impact.

Monitor how your competitors handle problems or negative publicity. Learning from their mistakes can help you better prepare for similar situations. Watch out for any new technology or equipment your competitors adopt. Falling behind in technological advances can pose a significant threat to competition.

Chapter 9:

Case Studies and Real-World Example

Social media marketing has become a cornerstone of digital marketing strategies, providing businesses with unparalleled opportunities to engage with their audience, build brand awareness, and drive sales. This chapter looks at real-world examples and case studies to demonstrate the power and viability of social media marketing across a variety of industries. and quickly spread across the globe.

Case Study 1: Coca-Cola's Share a Coke Campaign

Background: Coca-Cola's Share a Coke campaign was launched in Australia in 2011 and quickly spread around the world. The campaign involves replacing the Coca-Cola logo on the bottle with 150 of the most popular names in each country.

The Strategy: The campaign uses social media to encourage consumers to find bottles with their names on them and share photos using the hashtag #ShareaCoke.

Results:

Act: The campaign had over 500,000 photos shared on social media.

Advertising: Coca-Cola reported a 2% increase in sales in the United States after the campaign launched.

Brand Loyalty: The personal nature of the campaign fosters a connection between the customer and the brand.

Analysis: The success of the Share A Coke campaign highlights the effectiveness of personality and user-generated content in driving engagement and sales. By making customers feel special and encouraging them to share their experiences, Coca-Cola harnesses the power of social media virality.

Case Study 2: Airbnb's #WeAccept Campaign

Background: In response to global political and social unrest, Airbnb launched its #WeAccept campaign during the 2017 Super Bowl.

The Plan: The campaign includes a powerful Super Bowl ad and a commitment to provide short-term housing to 100,000 people in need over the next five years. Airbnb encourages users to share their acceptance stories on social media using the hashtag #WeAccept.

Results:

Feelings about the brand: This campaign significantly increased positive sentiment toward Airbnb because it linked the brand to social inclusion and responsibility.

Commitment: The hashtag #WeAccept generated a lot of attention, with thousands of shares and debates on social networks.

Impact: Airbnb has demonstrated its values, attracted more people and strengthened its image as a socially responsible company.

Analysis: Airbnb's campaign shows the importance of integrating social media marketing with the brand's core values. By solving relevant social problems and encouraging user engagement, brands can create meaningful connections with their audiences.

Case Study 3: Wendy's Twitter Roasts

Background: Wendy's has gained a reputation for its witty and often savage roasts on Twitter, engaging with both fans and competitors in a humorous and bold manner.

Strategy: Wendy's uses real-time engagement and a distinctive brand voice to respond to tweets, create viral content, and maintain an active presence on Twitter.

Results:

Follower Growth: Wendy's Twitter account has seen significant follower growth due to its entertaining and relatable content.Brand Awareness: The brand's unique approach has been widely covered in media, increasing its visibility.

Consumer Engagement: Wendy's has successfully fostered a community of engaged followers who eagerly anticipate its next tweet.

Analysis: Wendy's demonstrates the effectiveness of a strong, consistent brand voice in social media marketing. By embracing humor and direct engagement, the brand has created a memorable and relatable online persona.

Case Study 4: GoPro's User-Generated Content

Background: GoPro, a company known for its action cameras, has built its marketing strategy around user-generated content.

Strategy: GoPro encourages its users to share their adventure videos on social media using the hashtag #GoPro. The company regularly features the best content on its own social media channels, creating a cycle of content generation and sharing.

Results:

Content Volume: The campaign has resulted in a vast library of high-quality, authentic content.

Community Building: GoPro has fostered a strong community of users who actively engage with the brand and each other.

Brand Loyalty: Featuring user content strengthens the bond between GoPro and its customers, driving brand loyalty.

Analysis: GoPro's strategy highlights the value of user-generated content in social media marketing. By leveraging the creativity and enthusiasm of its users, GoPro has created a sustainable and highly engaging content ecosystem

Chapter 10:
Conclusion

Effective social media marketing is no longer just an optional part of modern business practices, but an essential part. In this book, we explore the essential elements, strategies, tools, and practical applications that define social media marketing success. From understanding the complexities of different platforms and producing engaging content, to keeping up with and staying ahead of emerging trends, the social media marketing landscape is dynamic and vast. The case studies and real-world examples presented demonstrate the power of creativity, authenticity, and strategic planning. They show how companies—from small startups to global giants—are using the power of social media to build brands, engage audiences, drive sales, and cultivate loyalty. These examples prove that effective social media marketing requires more than just presence; as we move into an ever-evolving digital world, marketers must remain flexible and look for new opportunities to innovate. The principles outlined in this book provide a powerful framework, but true success will come from a commitment to learning, experimentation, and continuous improvement. By adopting the strategic methods and insights shared in this book, businesses can not only navigate the complexities of social media marketing but thrive in a rapidly changing and competitive environment. As you apply these strategies to your work, remember that the key to a successful social media campaign is the ability to meaningfully communicate with your audience, tell your brand story in a compelling way, and create a positive experience for your customers and your business that creates long-term value.